Dad's Story Copyright @ 2016 Scott J Klausfelder
ISBN-13: 978-1530641291
ISBN-10: 1530641292
By Scott J Klausfelder
Copyrighted Material

# INTRODUCTION

It has been said that any man can be a father, but only certain fathers can be a true dad. I never really knew exactly what the phrase meant until I became a father and a dad.

I owe everything to God and my wife. How both of them have ever managed to put up with me is the greatest example of love and grace. I never knew I deserved unconditional love that I receive multiple times on a daily basis. That's when I knew I needed to start fresh with God and with my wife. I am grateful for Jesus for his faith, courage, strength, and for sacrificing his life for our sins that provided eternal life to me the day I gave my life to Jesus.

Every day I thank Jesus for all my blessings and my precious family. This is a dad's story.

# DEDICATION

*I dedicate this book to my father, my dad. He was a beautiful man that loved so many and believed in Jesus Christ and treating others the way they should have been treated. I miss you every day dad. But you are always with me.*

## CHAPTER 1

# MY DAD-MY HERO

Growing up I was more blessed than some of my friends. It wasn't due to having a lifestyle of the rich and famous because we definitely did not have that. It wasn't due to having little chores or responsibilities to just run around with my friends because that was definitely not the case. I was blessed because my brother and I spent a lot of time together each day with our dad. My father owned a family auto body business. The business was located on the same property of our house which gave us the opportunity to spend time with him every day.

Each day had a formal regiment to it. I always thought in part it was due to the military background and experience my father had during Vietnam War. I soon realized it was due to the contribution of his work ethic implored upon him by his family, his faith, his military training and personality. As a child growing up, especially during the summer months, it seemed like a dose of boot camp and prison in the best way possible! Each morning roll call was at 0700 or 7:00 am for most of us. If you made the mistake of sleeping through roll call, you soon realized what mattress acrobatics were as you were flipped off the bed onto the floor! Now don't get me wrong that was a great way to start your morning.

After we awoke, or were *awoken*, we got dressed and went to the dining room table for breakfast. We were greeted by a bowl of cheerios and a list of chores. During breakfast it wasn't the cheerios that gave us the energy to tackle the day ahead as it did for Clark Kent in the original Superman movie. We were not going to be flying through our chores with capes on just because we ate the Cheerios.

It was the prize of freedom that motivated us to complete the chore list, which usually included all the house work, the lawn and the garden. My mom went back to school to finish her degree in those days and it resulted in a lot of work for my brother and me. I am very proud of my mother for her strength to return to school and complete her education. I learned a few valuable lessons back then. I realized that only your true friends would help you finish the chores to break you free and attain freedom to do what we wanted.

For some reason my father planted a larger garden each year and said it was a great stress reliever to him. I beg to differ! The second thing I learned was a larger garden was NOT a stress reliever for me since I had the pleasure of pulling weeds and harvesting the crops. I still don't like gardens to this day. I was learning that hard work taught me true discipline.

But what I didn't understand at the time is that we didn't have a lot of money. My father provided for us the best way he could by ensuring we were nourished with our soul and body and we grew our own food.

I am convinced I would not have the work ethic I have today if it were not for my father and mother teaching us all they did at a young age. We were a family that loved, worked and played together.

Even with all the chores we had growing up having the opportunity to be part of a family business and learn a trade was an experience that was not replaceable. Not every child had the opportunity to crawl into trunks of large cars from the 60's and 70's to brush under coat which sure resembled tar everywhere. The fact that I could fit in the trunk of these cars with a 5 gallon can of undercoat was incredible. Coming out of the trunk I usually had more tar on me than the car but loved every minute of it to learn from my father.

It was an incredible experience to learn how to weld at the age of 9 and how to use a spray gun and paint my go-kart. This was my first taste of freedom. My father instilled discipline, hard work, love and freedom to live your life to the fullest.  I also realized I had the coolest dad in the world when he taught me how to drive at age 10.  It wasn't only the fun and cool stuff I remember, it was the fact that my dad took time from a busy day to make me a priority. We would have fun in everything we did as long as we were together.

My dad taught me vital things that shaped my character and made me the man I am today.  He stressed to always tell the truth, admit when you make mistakes and always look someone in the eye when you are talking to them.  A firm handshake and your word is all you need to show what kind of man you are in life. My dad was a very respectful and respected man.

I know I didn't fully understand the impact my dad was making on me at that young age. However, as the years went by I realized exactly what legacy my father built in myself and my brother.

# CHAPTER 2

# BUILDING THE FOUNDATION

Looking back over the years, one of the most difficult but most rewarding tasks that my father had our family embark upon was building a log home in the middle of farm land. My father decided to close the family business and move us to the country. I wish we had kept the business however moving to the country and working hard from dawn to dusk from spring to fall was quite the experience. Family and God always came first. This has shaped the man I am today. To love, give, provide, protect, teach and listen in a selfless way for others.

I learned a lot about construction and how a foundation of a house is the most critical part. If the footer is poured improperly or the cinder blocks are not installed correctly, the foundation will become weak and cannot support the house. I observed exactly what the process was from start to finish and realized that our lives are also built upon a foundation. If we really think about that statement for a moment the essentials of our faith are upon Christ. Everything we believe and act upon is directly related to our faith with Jesus and he is our foundation that we build our lives upon.

Jesus used an example comparing a house built on sand and a house built on a rock. When the storms of life came upon the two houses the one built upon the sand couldn't withstand the storm and collapsed. However the house built upon the rock withstood the storm. Jesus is our rock and our foundation, as we all had two categories of houses that Jesus talked about. The question of which house you want built upon which foundation becomes obvious. We all want a house built on a rock but we need to realize that rock is our relationship in Christ to implement the necessary building blocks in the lives of our children to be certain their house will withstand the storms of life.

This is a statement that I know my parents thought of and acted upon. It was evident growing up that the Bible was taught as well as the importance of a church family. I do remember how involved we were as a family in church but also living the love of Christ through relationships, friends, neighbors, and community. I remember as a young child this love took many beautiful shapes with a diverse group of people that shared love through Christ.

While we lived in the country, there was a motorcycle gang that lived next to us. This was back in the 70's and I know some of them had trouble with the law. But nonetheless there was a young boy close to my age that was my friend despite his situation. I also remember various people living with my family over the years mostly due to challenges they had with their own families. This was the love of Christ that was the basis of our foundation in life and radiated through our lives in many relationships.

As we reflect upon the other essential building blocks we see how faith and love go hand in hand. But also character develops through this foundation. Therefore the foundations that are laid in our lives have a great impact in the lives of our children. We need to ask ourselves as parents, "What foundation are we building in our children?"

# CHAPTER 3

# THE TEENAGE YEARS

Growing up I thought my transition from a child to a young man went somewhat smooth but my parents may have had a different opinion. I think every son gives his father an opportunity to express patience and grace through various adventures. That was definitely me and my brother. Everyday had to have some excitement in it. The various ways we chose to find it perhaps weren't always the best. Looking back no one ever got seriously injured or arrested, we truly saw how well God helped my father handle every situation that arose.

Some of our fun adventures included racing bikes and poor judgment with the lawn mower.  For some reason I do believe my love and passion for motorsports and speed came from my father.  He was full of life.  When I turned thirteen he saw an opportunity to not only bond with his son but also to keep his son from embarking upon adventures that had greater consequences when enticed by the influence of my peers.  While I was away at camp Rockwood that summer, I came home to a big surprise!  My father purchased a 1967 Mustang for me.

    He was not just handing over the keys to a thirteen year old boy who knew how to drive.  He had chosen this car because it was totaled or shall I say it became rather personal with a telephone pole. The condition of the car didn't matter to my father or me. What DID matter was the potential the car had was similar to the potential that my father saw in me. The time and expense wasn't relevant. What was important was the value of the time we spent together which was priceless.

I must truly admit the car became a lengthy project which gave me quality time with my father. My father was there each step of the way and taught me so much. He taught me about the auto body trade but also about the importance of having patience, working hard and doing a job correctly the first time.  These fond memories are exactly the same memories that I want to replicate with my children.  I am not certain that my kids all share the same love for cars that I have but the opportunity to spend time with them involved in any project is a blessing.

My advice to all fathers who are reading this book would be to take the time now and really get to know your children. What they love, what they fear, what their passions are.  And when you truly know your children you can provide true guidance and be a dad.  I am grateful that my father did this for me and genuinely cared about me as a person, not just his son but making sure I would grow up into the man he and God expected.

# CHAPTER 4

# TAKING A STAND

I remember my father being a patient man who was firm and clear with his communication. I believe he always made his point and despite the situation he remained calm at all times. To me, he was the epitome of strength, courage, control and protector.

I remember coming home one day after having a collision with my mom's car. My father was less than pleased with the appearance of the car which sustained damage to the front end. I learned a couple of things that day. First, watch how closely you follow the person in front of you especially when you sneeze and don't realize they came to a complete stop. Second, my father remained in complete control despite the situation. I then came to realize it was because I was going to be fixing the car with his help. My father made it clear that I was responsible for my actions. I had to pay for the parts to repair the car but he graciously helped me fix the car. Now this repair wasn't the same bonding experience that my mustang was but I learned to take responsibility for my actions. I realized my father's message to me was to take responsible for my actions. He gave me the tools and strength to convert my wrongs into rights.

As I look back over the years, one thing I remember was the need to take a stand for responsibility. It didn't always matter whether the situation that happened was a good or bad one. What really made the difference was how it was handled and what action to resolve it was taken.

My father was always open to giving us more responsibility which continued to build our character. This made my brother and I realize that there were consequences of not handling more responsibility. When responsibility and accountability is exercised, true leadership is developed.

I am grateful for the opportunities my father gave me over the years. It not only made me who I am today but it also helped me realize the level of trust that he had in me. This is what we need to teach our children. They need to take a stand and have ownership over their actions and accept the consequences and act on responsibility.

These principles are challenged in the world we live in. It is too easy in our society to evade consequence for our actions rather than be accountable for them and correcting them.

# CHAPTER 5

# CHANGE IN SOCIETY

As I've grown I have seen our society shift where responsibility, accountability, and work ethic has weakened. Nowadays you see more children quitting school or college, accept government funded programs when they have the ability to work and contribute to society.

It seems there are too many law suits filed just because you can. If you spilled hot coffee on yourself and you know the coffee is hot, how is that someone else's fault? Why can't society take responsibility for their consequences and love thy brother and realize how your actions will impact someone else. Or is it just greed now? In my opinion, the worst is all the failed marriages. Failed marriages come from lack of foundation, faith, love of God and commitment. The children are the ones that suffer the most as the foundation is then removed and lives are shattered.

As a society that shaped different values and ethics many years ago we have allowed ourselves to live with little consequence and in the process have failed to teach our children what true responsibilities and consequences look like. Developing discipline and perseverance to embrace the responsibilities we have been entrusted with is not an option in raising our children and it must begin with ourselves as parents.

Imagine the integrity our children would develop if our society embraced the same values and ethics we watched back in the days of "Leave it to Beaver " and "Little House on the Praire."  Look at the quality of a family life and community that was demonstrated and I believe acted upon in real life years ago.  We need to ask ourselves, "Where have we gone wrong?"

As a country founded on Christian values and ethics which kept God at the center of our lives, we have to realize the negative effects we have encountered as a society that no longer keeps God at the center of life. We have removed God from our schools, courts, and workplace. We have accepted liberal views that are being taught to our children in public schools. Our decay as a society is the result of our consequences.

When God is not in our home and hearts, Satan realizes the philosophy of attacking the shepherd and the flock will scatter. Once the sheep are isolated they become easy prey. This can be seen through promiscuity, greed, substance abuse and everything evil. That is NOT what we want for our children.

We need to take a stand for Christ and his place in our lives. We must reclaim our families for him. Fathers must exercise their God given role in being the spiritual leader and provider of their family. It is time to take a stand for our faith the welfare of our children.

# CHAPTER 6

# THE CHALLENGE

One of the hardest things I saw my father be challenged with was implementing his spiritual and personal convictions to his children in a fallen world but did so with his daily actions and grace. I have no doubt that we knew those convictions and ethics growing up. Growing up, spending a lot of time at home and with my dad at the business, we realized that the world doesn't embrace the same Christian values that we did.

My father realized not all people shared the same Christian values as he did with some of the business relationships that developed. My father and his servant's heart made him vulnerable be taken advantage of numerous times over the years but he never changed who he was and his faith remained strong.

As a child growing up and realizing how dishonest or untrustworthy people are really jaded the application of love thy neighbor and thy enemy.

How my father handled those situations really taught us what a faith filled life really looks like. My mother displayed the same character traits as my father did. I truly remember that nothing ever got past her. She was incredibly smart and ensured that I would be told of any of my wrong doings. She was the nurturer and also the disciplinarian when needed. Whenever curfew was broken, she was on the other side of the screen door no matter what time of night!

I firmly believe we learn many valuable lessons from our parents. The same challenges that they faced in raising us we actually encounter today.

I think society has decayed more today than when I was a child and will continue to decay as time goes on. Family values have been put on the back burner compared to how they were when I grew up. We were expected to work hard, love family, love our neighbors, friends and strangers. We lived with doors left unlocked and knew it was safe. Today, trust has been questioned within our society and not filled with love but rather greed. That fact alone should motivate every father who has Jesus as his Lord to embrace the blessing of his role and the responsibility of raising his children and remind them that it begins with Jesus Christ and family.

So the question becomes, what is preventing fathers from doing the job they need to? Well I believe there are many factors that contribute to the lack of leadership from fathers in today's society.

Liberalism has emasculated fathers from assuming their God given roles. Fathers don't have the respect of the society, their spouses or their children as they need to in order to serve as the leader and provider of their family.

The reality is that the impact of fathers not assuming the role they needed to has already impacted their children who are adults today. We have men who become fathers yet have no idea what a dad is really supposed to do. Whether their father was absent or had no faith in God and Jesus, his role has already made a negative impact for the next generation.

The blessing of multi-generational relationships is not as evident today as it was years ago in both church and family. There is a void in how we as a society view our elders, rather than embracing their lifelong experiences we put them in senior community houses or nursing homes.

As a society we are to blame for the loss of valuable wisdom being passed down to the next generation. We need to break the cycle and restore the family which will restore the family of families. It has to begin with fathers reaching out to other fathers and disciplining them through God's word and life experiences. Fathers need to claim their authority given by God for his children.

Imagine what our society would look like if this was to happen. Imagine the legacy that will be passed on to the next generation. It is time to take a stand in the name of Christ. It is time for fathers to impart Godly wisdom in their children and teach them the truth which only comes from God's word. Our children need to know what a true relationship with Jesus looks like and how that relates to our relationships with other family members. It is time to say no to society and bring our nation under God back to God.

One of my saddest days of my life was losing my father unexpectedly when I was twenty one years old. I was devastated. I know my father is still around and looking over his family but to have one more face to face conversation with him would be incredible. Never take life for granted. The lord gives us each day for his purpose.

# CHAPTER 7

# RETURN TO SIMPLICITY

I remember growing up at home not having air conditioning or cable TV. I remember using fans during the humidity and heat of the summer. Rabbit ears and tin foil was all you needed to get your VHF and UHF channels in. We had 1 phone in the house with a rotary dial. We didn't seem to be missing anything. Our fireplace provided heat and we didn't get into video games or computers.

Now don't get me wrong, at times I wanted what my friends had with all the luxuries of life. However, I learned that true quality of family life isn't found in material things or the latest technology.

Quality family life is found in the blessings from God which is in relationships with one another and enjoying his creation. Some of the best memories I have from my childhood involved spending time with family members and doing the simplest things together. It didn't matter if we were raking leaves, cutting firewood or preparing dinner.

The time spent enjoying each other and physical work was truly priceless. I remember the phrase "I'm bored" was never an option. Time had few demands upon us outside of our chores or family time. We realized that personal communication outweighed short phone calls. The need to speak face to face with someone really made relationships genuine. Almost everywhere you went, you physically and verbally interacted with people not machines.

The personal touch in every aspect of life was seen and experienced. It didn't make a difference whether you went shopping or went to the bank you had a personal encounter with someone. Times have certainly changed. You can actually have little personal contact with most things in everyday life. Technology has created benefits in life however it has now invaded our privacy and placed an overwhelming demand of our time.

Now it is possible to text, email and video chat all at the same time. Having unrestricted access to people at any time has allowed people to not utilize personal verbal communication. Respect has diminished that is a valid point proven by the statements made on Facebook. I see people hiding behind their keyboards or keypads expressing every feeling rather than the verbal personal method that God created. People lack personal skills and confidence by not having to communicate verbally. The need to work out confrontations in person has also been alleviated and you now see what is called cyber bullying.

I'm not saying we should live in the dark ages, but I am saying we must emphasize God and restore the context of personal communication. Personal communication and touch enhances the quality of every relationship in the family and community.

Stop and think about this for a moment, if everyone took 30 days and deprived ourselves of all electronics, we would have to develop better communication skills and connections to

God, peace and family. Is that really deprivation? Too often we hear people complain that they are so stressed and never have time to do anything. I believe that has to do with technology and social media while never just sitting and listening to God.

Listening and talking would take a new shape. Personal time together would actually involve one-on-one conversations with few to no distractions. Reading or playing games would take hold and bring laughter and unity. Getting off the couch and going outside to enjoy God's creation would take place as well as help us with our health to exercise more.

Time is a blessing in reality. God gives us each day to enjoy one another and serve him. Distractions place an unhealthy demand of our time and deprive us of enjoying relationships with each other and especially him.

We must desire to want to build and strengthen our relationships, first in God, second in our family and third within the community. Discipline and desire usually don't work together. One overwhelms the other and it is usually desire that wins that battle.

So my challenge to every father who reads this book is to take your role as the leader of your family before the world does. I have noticed how we all have good intentions but give into the temptation of worldly distractions. Leading the wellness of our family would be much easier living in a cabin in the woods with no people and no electronics. However as nice as that sounds, it is not practical. We must not only grow where God leads us but also we must reach out to those around us.

# CHAPTER 8

# THE CALL

About 10 years ago I realized the calling the Lord had placed into my life as a Pastor. I felt excited and scared at the same time if that is possible. I realized that at my age while working fulltime in the automotive field and supporting my family, answering the call to ministry would be a challenge in many ways. First the academic challenge. I had completed Vo-tech school with a diploma in Automotive Technology and then went on to additional training over the years and various ways.

Going to college even part time would be difficult. But to attain a degree that would be the first step to Seminary proved to be a long costly endeavor. Thankfully the Lord opened a door to training that would not only equip me as a Pastor but could be done on a smaller scale and not hinder my work or family time.

The 2nd challenge to my call in ministry was the question of why me? Even though I grew up in a Christian family that went to church every Sunday involved in various forms of ministry and lived my life by God I still questioned why me?

However when I was 15 or 16, I saw youth group as a great way to meet girls and since I had my own car I could share my freedom with them. At that time we didn't realize how special youth group was but when I realize what that group gave me I am overwhelmed with the opportunity it gave me to connect with Christ at such an early age. So before I realized that this was the beginning of a journey that lasted 10 years for me. I lived more for myself and freedom than I did for Christ in those days. It wasn't until I was on the West Mesa of Albuquerque New Mexico, that God got my attention when I was 25 years old and I knew it was time to stop running but rather time to listen and get it all right with him.

I gave my life to him soon after that and the journey has never been the same since. I know I struggled with the sense of not being worthy of the call God had given me. My past in my opinion had disqualified me. However I soon began to understand what grace, forgiveness and unconditional love was all about. Although I gave that to others, it took me awhile to realize God was giving it to me and I was worthy.

As I began this new journey in my life my wife joined me with a new beginning herself and was a huge support all these years since. I have learned many things over the years and quite a few from the results of mistakes. However God will use everything whether bad or good to lead us towards glory for him.

    This is what motivated me to make changes in how I view not only my life and the precious gift of time but also the impact that I am making in the lives of others. We all must honestly ask ourselves this question. "Am I truly using each minute of each hour of each day to glorify God?" If I am not living for him then who am I living for? If we center our lives with our personal desires we will live a shallow unproductive life for the Kingdom of God.

    The world has become a great place with technology but the false need of constantly needing to be self-focused and entertained has robbed us of finding the blessing found in family and relationships. Texting and ordering everything on-line has eliminated the need for personal communication. This is where the family has come under attack and balance needs to be restored. Technology is great when used in proper context. God has created us to be in community with one another. The family is at the center of the community with Jesus at the head. This is the order of priority in our lives and this is where we must all begin, if we desire to live the abundant life that Jesus described, we must all evaluate our relationship with him. If that isn't in place in our lives, everything else in our lives will have little meaning and our desires will rule our intentions.

To answer the call that God has given each and every one of us we must first ask ourselves these very important questions. Have I asked Jesus to be Lord of my life? Have I repented of all my sins and is anything preventing me of having a solid relationship with him? Am I completely committed to Jesus? When we can truly say yes to all of these questions, then we are ready to answer the call. Let the journey begin!

# CHAPTER 9

# I HAVE FAILED

It has been said that a man can value success by his failures. This is an interesting statement to me. If this statement was true solely on its literal application I would be a CEO of some multi-billion dollar corporation.

However, I believe there is another application of that saying and here is how it applies to my life experience. I have failed at many things in my life and in almost every area of my life as well. I have had failures during my school years and within all of my relationships.

I have failed in my vocation, my ministry, my marriage and definitely as a father while raising my kids. Wow! If we are truly honest with ourselves perhaps our failures out number our successes. The key point that the statement is really making is not to identify failure as a strong hold to prevent us from success in every area of life but to use failure as a learning application towards developing perseverance and wisdom. I have honestly learned from my failures and have not allowed them to prevent me from success. One thing I have learned is to not only admit my failures and short comings but strive to reach the goal despite of them.

    I realized this early in life when I

thought I had some athletic talent as a child I tried almost every sport and realized I could have been successful had I tried and committed to a sport. My failures were not giving it 100 percent and trying to participate; but rather I chose a different path that was not what gave me the peace of Christ that I have today. I believe we all can admit to multiple failures in our lives. The question is how did you apply them to who you are today?

To me, being honest and failing in front of my family teaches them that I am human and not perfect. This builds a strong sense of self as a person to know we are all human with faults.

Some of us have put those failures in the same category as self-worth and added any verbal abuse that occupied in life to fully encapsulate us in a continual sense of low self-esteem. Other people have used those failures and other harmful short comings in life to propel us towards success in accomplishing our goals and actually giving us a high self-esteem.

This becomes a delicate balance to not allow pride to become a dangerous thing. As a father I have realized the importance of allowing my children to see the role of failure in my life. How I handled failure is crucial in helping them address it in their lives as well. I honestly believe that none of my children struggle with low self-esteem and this approach to failure is part of the reason why.

As parents we must embrace everything that life gives us from a view similar to what the book of James shares with us in regard to counting it pure joy whenever we encounter various trials in our lives. Because these trials allow us to develop perseverance, and perseverance helps us to exercise and strengthen our faith. We need to realize that God is in control of everything. We need to have faith that he will get us through each and every failure and trial that we encounter.

As a result we come above the failure or trial and stronger in our faith. We also realize that our sense of self-worth comes only from God himself. These are exactly the things we need to be applying in our lives and teaching our children. As with many things in life, teaching comes in various ways. Not for a written instruction that has a limited application but practical living in obedience to God's word is the best form of teaching. As parents our actions must outweigh our words to truly impact our children for generations to come.

# CHAPTER 10

# A SERVANT'S HEART

A short time ago I was going through some papers and stumbled across a folder that had a copy of the sermon given at my father's funeral. I had to take a moment and read it. The Pastor really knew my father well and focused on what a servant's heart really looked like.

He shared the example given by Jesus as a servant that serves from the heart and that was true with my father. My father had a genuine love for people that I am sure the Lord gave him. I know that he loved to help people. I remember my father not just telling us to put the needs of others before our own but showing us exactly how that is done.

It has to begin in our heart. The heart can be a fickle thing at times and make you do things you may or may not want to do.

As for my father he found total and complete joy in helping people in various ways. He was heavily involved with the church, his family, owned an auto business, and volunteering with the local ambulance squad. His complete involvement in these areas really created a lot of opportunities for him to help and reach others with the love of Christ.

I believe God organizes every opportunity he gives us to glorify him and live out Christ's love. My father seized every opportunity to serve others. His actions always out spoke his words. This was the key factor that really taught us about true servant hood.

So many times in life we all have good intentions that develop into actions. But for a lot of folks those good intentions seem to get buried by the demands of our time whether directly inflicted or not. Think about this point. How many times have you been given the opportunity to make a difference in someone's life and maybe initially acted upon it but soon realized you had other priorities that you allowed to overcome your actions?

If we are truly honest with ourselves, we are all guilty of doing this at one time in our life. We have to ask ourselves, as parents, "What does this teach our children?" Are good intentions enough? Is a halfhearted action to a good intention what it takes to show what a true servant's heart is? Did Jesus in the upper room just wash Peter's feet and say "Alright fellows, listen to me, you all have dirty stinky feet except now for Peter. Do you get the message of what I am trying to demonstrate for you? Do I really have to wash all your feet?"

This isn't what Jesus did. He

demonstrated a few things by the action he performed that day in the upper room. The first was love with no boundaries. There were no limits to the love He demonstrated that day, in his years of ministry and especially what he did on the cross for each of us.

The second was the master to servant context. Think about this for a moment. The foot washing job back in that time and culture was usually delegated to a servant. You would not see someone with higher authority or regard doing a job like that. I assume his disciples at first were shocked that Jesus would lower himself to that level.

However the disciples learned a lot that day about a true servant's heart. The disciples learned about true friendship no matter the hierarchy.

The third was the true reality of the fact that we all walk in a sinful world and the need to wash ourselves daily of the sins that cling to us and repent. Jesus made this point clear by the actions he performed that day and on the cross. He made it possible for each of us to be cleansed daily and start fresh with him each day.

The example that Jesus made as a servant is exactly what we need to be teaching our children. We need to be not just telling our children to share the love of Christ with others but we need to be living it out in every opportunity that God presents us with.

This requires not only good intentions but actions that speak louder than your words. We must involve our children in every part of every opportunity we have to help others.

There is this indescribable joy you experience when you help someone. I saw this joy in my father and have experienced it in my own life. When you are living your life in the context of servant hood, I truly believe you experience the abundant life that only comes through a relationship with Jesus Christ.

# CHAPTER 11

# A FATHER'S CHILDREN

I read a book once about the relationship between a father and daughter and how unique and important the context of that relationship truly is. I learned how unique the love that a daughter and father share. The book was a great resource of information written by a doctor who is a woman. Her perspective was great and I made some changes in how I love my daughter and the structure I implement to raise her as a young woman of God.

I read about the challenge of raising a daughter in a fallen corrupt world. By the time I was done the book I was ready to homeschool my daughter, not let her ever date a boy and arrange her marriage when I found the right man.

I may sound a little old fashioned, overbearing and protective by my previous statement, however my point is evident. Raising a daughter in today's society is hard. Just about everything in society points to materialism, sex, lack of responsibility and disrespect.

Everything you don't want your daughter doing and since they have removed the morals and ethics rooted in the Judeo Christian beliefs that once governed our society, our efforts to raise our kids according to God's word are challenged. We must take a stand for Christ at home, at work and in our community.

We have two sons and raising them is different than raising a daughter because as a dad you are more protective over your daughter. We're raising our sons to act upon the godly foundation that we have built and instilled upon them. We want our sons to become Godly men of integrity to be the protectors of their spouses and families.

Our children need to see our faith lived out and intertwined in all parts of our lives. We all must live in this world and as much as we want to shelter our children from the pain and cruelty seen in this world we must show the love of Christ, teach them how to love others, walk by faith not by sight and live by God's word. The power of prayer is essential for each day. Pray often and listen patiently. When you truly listen you will hear God and be ready to respond when God tells you to act.

# CHAPTER 12

# THE DATING GAME

As a father I kept telling myself that it will be years from now until my daughter will start dating. I fully believed that 21 was an appropriate age for my daughter to begin dating and my wife thought 16 was fine. I knew I had lost this battle before it began. I decided it was time to discuss what the dating expectations and rules were going to be. My daughter agreed to my standard in boys.

Well it wasn't long until she liked candidate #1 as we will call him. Now this young man was rather timid and intelligent. He was very polite and respectful. He seemed harmless. I had come up with my own test that I was going to use to see if this young man was going to be a concern for me or not.

I am big on handshakes that are firm and with full eye contact during conversations. I reached out to this young man and grasped his hand in a very firm handshake and pulled him into me while looking him straight in the eyes.

Needless to say he broke eye contact quickly and looked down at the ground. I knew that moment the power of intimidation had this young man calling me sir and displaying full respect. I remember having a full discussion of how my princess will be no one's conquest and how no one will hurt her. I love the look when I tell them I'm not afraid to go back to prison. Of course they don't know that I mean my time spent in prison was serving in prison ministry for years. But I leave that up to them to figure out.

Yes fear and intimidation serve a valuable purpose at times. The two previous boyfriends overcame their fear of me because once I was sure they were respectful of my daughter and my family, I showed them love and welcomed them into my home as I am a man of God but also a protector of my family.

It is a wonderful feeling to be able to call him son. My encouragement to my daughter has been this, "If your boyfriend truly loves God he will know how to truly love you."

## CHAPTER 13

# MY BLENDED FAMILY

Many years ago the Lord placed upon my heart the desire to reach out to young people. I loved teaching Sunday school to very young children. I love how genuine they are in their love of God and other people. As time went on I felt the calling to help teens and serve in youth ministry.

I knew that I had enjoyed the youth group in my church growing up and felt that God had gifted me in many ways to really relate to the teens and teach them God's work.

At times my adventurous side led us all into interesting experiences. But what I really learned was that you don't need to be a superstar or professional athlete to really reach kids. You just have to love Jesus and his love will radiate from you into the lives of those around you.

I didn't have to be cool for kids to like me. I had to be me, be real and love them as they were and who they became. Genuine love was all I needed to show. It's amazing how much love is lacking in the world and how much we all need it. That is what God is trying to tell us.

Over the years we ended up with many "adopted" sons and daughters. My wife and I became 2nd parents to many kids.

I have fond memories of all the blessings the Lord has given me in the relationships with these kids. A lot of these young people have grown up and are married with kids of their own.

It is really encouraging to have contact with them and be told that I made a difference in someone's life. It makes the challenges and the loss of my hair worthwhile. I'm now at that point in life as to what the next step in ministry looks like for me.

Due to a roller coaster accident with the youth group, I have become limited with helping the younger kids because of my physical limitations, not my spirit. I see myself now raising my teenage kids and our "adopted ones." I am truly a blessed man. I am father #2 to my daughter's best friend and really enjoy the heart felt talks we have. I also have been blessed with a third daughter who is older and facing the challenges of adult life. She is a tower of strength to overcome all she has been challenged with. She now is my administrative assistant helping me with my business. She is talented, funny, a great mother and a beautiful person.

What amazes me is being a good listener, showing support of their decisions and loving them unconditionally and seeing the impact that makes. Not to mention me being a rather large man who can intimidate any of their boyfriends to be their protector and give them a true sense of security. I truly thank God for these girls and am a very blessed father and dad. I will always look over them and protect them from bad and teach them how loved and special they are because God loves them.

I realize the responsibility I have been given and will do my best to make a difference in their lives that will glorify God and enable them to pass on the legacy to their children one day. It is interesting how the relationship changes with my son's.

Now I have included my daughter's boyfriend in this group. In fact I have recently allowed him to stop calling me sir but call me Dad. The same qualities of a genuine relationship exist between me and my sons. However what differs is raising them to be men of God and leaders of their family and husbands of integrity to their wives. I know the boys are young but this training started early in life. I have learned that they want the same interests in life that I have and will resemble not only my good qualities but my not so good ones as well.

At times this can be rather overwhelming but the blessing of being a father comes with great responsibility. I also believe that fathers face unique trails and challenges in our role which at times can hinder us or if we rely on God can make us stronger.

This is why I encourage fathers to unite and open up to God's message to lead your family and raise your children. Don't expect nor allow the government, or our schools nor our society to assume this role. Be men of integrity and take a stand now for our kids and the next generation.

# CHAPTER 14

# MY GROWING FAMILY

I have realized in my life that your true family is never limited to those of blood or material relations. True family are those who realize God has placed with you for the road trip we call life. I know people come and go in our lives. Some are here for a short time some are here for this life and some for eternal life to come.

As I look back over the years my wife and we have opened our hearts and home to many people. I have realized we had such a wonderful privilege to make not only a difference in someone's life by providing for their physical needs such as food, clothes, shelter and health care but more importantly their spiritual needs.

I believe in divine appointment in my life. You meet someone and if you listen to the guidance of the Holy Spirit you realize there is a reason that you are talking with this person. It is exciting how God reveals his plan as a result of our obedience. All we do is share the love of Christ and our hope in him.

It is amazing how many people just want to experience that love and the hope it gives you to not only make it in this life but prepares you for the life to come. Through the years we have seen how powerful this love of Christ truly is. I have seen lives changed forever. It has been such a blessing to reach people with the power of the Gospel and see them love the Lord and life.

As time goes on God continues to grow us and our family. There are many things to be thankful for in life but the blessing of true friends and family is really the greatest joy.

# CHAPTER 15

# THE LOVE I RECEIVE

I knew my life was to serve God and share his message. What I didn't realize was the unconditional love I would receive in return. Not just from God but from those that God brought to me to help. I am humbly grateful for my gift to connect with God and to help those that have needed me. I have witnessed those healing and that fills my heart. My true love in this world is helping others and making them feel worthy of love. Allowing me to send that message makes me complete.

Through my trials and tribulations I didn't understand them at the time. It's the faith that kept me going. When I see what comes in front of me through faith is remarkable. There is a reason I'm here and why I have this message to share. Live by God's words, be faithful and loyal and the love will come in ways you never expected.

The lessons from God and my father are what helped me realize my calling to God and helping others any way I possibly can. I am also honored to say they shaped me from a father to a dad.

# ABOUT THE AUTHOR

Scott J Klausfelder was born and raised in Quakertown, Pennsylvania. He studied Ministry/Theology at Antioch School. He is the Senior Pastor at The Gathering. He is the owner and operator of Klausfelder Kustom Kars. He is married with three beautiful children currently residing in Richlandtown, Pennsylvania. When he's not in church or working at his shop, he is spending his time counseling those in need and helping them find peace and love through Jesus Christ.

Made in the USA
Charleston, SC
14 April 2016